For The Sport of Laughter for all

Sherman A. Jones
Editor-in-Chief

Poetic And Crazy

Humor, Philosophy, & Poem

Author: *Sherman A. Jones*

- Summer 2015

- Cbookspublishing and Bookstore

Poetic And Crazy

Cbookspublishing and Bookstore
619 Copeland Dr.
Cedar Hill, Texas 75104
www.cbookspublishing.com

ISBN: 978-0-9849733-8-5

Library of Congress Control Number: 2015915699

b

TABLE OF CONTENT

c

Chapter II ⟵

Chapter III —

Chapter IV —

e

Chapter V ⟵

Chapter VI ⟵

Chapter VIII ⟵

Chapter IX ⟵

h

Chapter X ←

Chapter XI ←

Chapter XII ⟵

About the Author

The cliparts of this book came from Microsoft Word.

Editor's Notes

Two notable quotes to highlight the editor's note:

"We all make mistakes, have struggled, and even regret things in our past. But you are not your mistakes, you are not your struggles, and you are here NOW with the power to shape your day and your future." — Steve Maraboli

---

"But what if I make a mistake? Will asked. Gilan threw back his head and laughed. 'A mistake? One mistake? You should be so lucky. You'll make dozens! I made four or five on my first day alone! Of course, you'll make mistakes. Just don't make any of them twice. If you do mess things up, don't try to hide it. Don't try to rationalize it. Recognize it and admit it and learn from it. We never stop learning, none of us." — John Flanagan

---

Editor's Notes Continuum

Poetic & Crazy, in the continuum of the present, borrows from this author's book (*Poetry and Beyond)* rewriting much that publication. *Poetry and Beyond* was written before this author acquired a degree of knowledge as how to write. The arrayed grouping of poems and philosophical thoughts in *Poetic & Crazy* will compliment and will use some works from the book, *Poetry and Beyond*, at the same time adding and

I

upgrading the quality of work. Highlights throughout this book, *Poetic & Crazy,* will be of the following: (1) Humor, (2) varying poetic styles, and (3) philosophy.

This is a philosophical quote of mine: *"Learning is an endless task of stultification— with none ever grown, but with an ever growing—despite the acquired"*~Sherman A. Jones. The expansion points of this publication are in the mandatory improvement in this author's ability to communicate with the art of writing. After acquiring a master's degree in Higher Education, this author looked over previously published materials realized a rework of these publications must be first on his priority list of things to do. This following poem expresses what *Poetic and Crazy* is all about in my now task of madness corrections:

Trying in vain to re-work
    my old failures, trying
    to collate the wreckage,
    the papered proof, the pile-up
    of so much gone wrong.
    Trying to make it into
    Something stable, like a plow,
    Something useful, like a plow
    Turning over clods of dirt
    Behind two stoic beasts
    Who couldn't care less
    If they lived or died.
    Slogging through a field
    Of burdock and Queen Anne's lace,

I have to stop and laugh. Ha!
I can make neither plow to drag
Nor yoke to drag it, I can, in fact,
Make nothing truly useful, nothing
That could turn one lump
Of solemn earth upon its back. (Stock, 2008)

The sheer thought to the name of this book, *Poetic & Crazy*, is a launch in the direction of amusement. As the story goes:

Mama's hot potato was ripe and ready for the stealing. It would be sweet if one did not get caught. It would be bitter-too-sweet for all, if Mama found out—whether anyone told or not! At least, we die with a belly full.

Poetic & Crazy is full of great amusement and is entertaining—sometimes off the grid; at the same time, the philosophical reaches into the soul expresses and questions the very essence of living occasionally. Is this a tragedy, or is this joy? It has been stated:

Plato, for instance, suggested that we find ludicrous or ridiculous those who lack self-knowledge (e.g., those who think they are better off than they actually are), and that we derive amusement from such misfortunes or absurdities (Morreall 1983). Similarly, in his allusion to humor in Poetics, Aristotle suggested that people derive amusement from the weaknesses or misfortunes of others as long as they are not too painful or destructive (Halliwell 1998 [1986], cited in Ferguson & Ford, 2008, p. 288).

As a stand-a-long of the included, enough is enough coming from the editor— turning now the page.

Notes

1. Stock, D. (2008). Rewrite. Dialectical Anthropology, 32 (4), 383. doi:10.1007/s10624-009-9084-y

2. Ferguson, M. A., & Ford, T. E. (2008). Disparagement humor: A theoretical and empirical review of psychoanalytic, superiority, and social identity theories. Humor: International Journal Of Humor Research, 21(3), 283-312. doi:10.1515/HUMOR.2008.014

Introduction

[*This book,* **Poetic, & Crazy,** *is a rewrite of the book,* **Poetry and Beyond**, *by this author. This book incorporates much of the knowledge this author acquired after writing the first of several books before getting his present held master's degree in Higher Education. This before stated will now take us to some of finest writings and thoughts ever pinned to paper*].

"When the whole world is crazy, it doesn't pay to be sane."
– *Terry Goodkind*

The magic of **"Crazy"** will sprout through this book to all out laughter. When there is not outright laughter, there will be as for the coming of you (my audience) a moment for pause with a gleeful eye searching for in between punch that stop the destruction of a work of art.

In the composition of poetic change, there — as if visually perceiving a butterfly in flight— is, and will be, the serene and stunning escalating to the burst of a stitch! On and after the introduction there will be the included clipart graphic enrich many of the punch lines for your <u>perceptions and interpretations</u>. What is it: a butterfly or a bat? The graphics help <u>augment, deepen, and enrich</u> the philosophical and poetic appreciations. Altogether, the flight

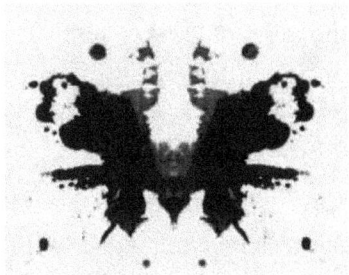

of the butterfly could be it's own self-contained interpretable, but the state to print consummates a composition juxtaposing the imperfections of life. Believe it or not, this shared plenary is in all contrasted similarities that make life crazy without the incoming poetic or philosophical. In other words, the crazy is the contained chapters that we are about to read, but most of the importations are already of our essence.

Whether or not, some optically discern a malevolent wonder or a wondrously malicious blonder as an inner or an outer contextual; each chapter of this book will be playing on such sundry words and phrases. This is the same as the enchanted flight of the butterfly that expresses the author's sentiments amidst the jocosity, crazy, and sultry words of philosophy and poetry. Breathtakingly, it is those of the above cause life to summarize to a no full or a no terminus comprehension that can never reach beyond the thinkable. The introduction of the unthinkable is never meant to offbeat or imbalanced the calibers head, but the intended for the reader, in the all out crazy, many ticklers for the hunger of the inner desiring niceties. [*Off-the-Beat*] Even dew drops turn spider webs into delicate oeuvres that astound the mind's ocular perceiver becomes poetic in the midst of nature's illimitable possibilities. Straightway we inundate to the undomesticated. Is this Philosophical or is this Poetic? Is this humor or is this just crazy? Chapters 1 through 10 are yours for the discerning.

"My brain is divided into two butterflies, and both are in love with your rose-shaped heart. If you've got the garden, I've got my whole life." — *Jarod Kintz,*

Theses chapters artistry, in the following, are of a profundity accenting the philosophical, poetic, and humorous for the purpose of bring out the craziness of self-reflections. This is the vicissitude wrapped in flesh transmuting a form of communication that says, "Gotcha!" That instantaneous tricked, tickled moment in time humors the beginning of complexity. Boredom is the world-weariness opposite being excitingly crazy. Philosophy is the passed stride phasing in the gradual transmuting dimensions of the incoming delight of artistic fullness. In the crazy and bizarre of human's constitutions, the dialectical undoes the affixed moves one to the next in an endeavor attempting to unravel the mystery of the poetic sempiternal. As stated from *A Joking Matter*:

> A minister woke up on a beautiful Sunday morning and decided to squeeze in a round of golf before services. St. Peter observed the man headed for the golf course and gave God a nudge. "He should be punished for this," God said, OK, just watch."
>
> The minister proceeded to play the best golf of his life. His club selection was precise, and he hit every shot perfectly. He was shooting par for the first time. "I thought you were going to punish him," said St. Peter. "Just watch," said God.
>
> The minister continued to play flawless golf, and on the 18th hole he shot a hole-in-one. "What kind

of punishment is this?" complained St. Peter. "Just think about it, said God. "Whom can he tell?" (Heim, 2003).

All of the following is from the hilarious to make crazy; rather than, the included from the crazy to make funny. And then again this too is a matter of interpretation. Therefore, the heart can be aware, and at the same time, struck with an inserted immaterial perception in the poetic blends and bounds of sane and insanity causing a reasonable convergence. Who knows! Another seeing a smile sees the other smiling can interpret as crazy. In the crossover, there will be many doubtful occasions for and against either comical or dim-witted, poetic or crazy, theoretical or realistic. The converging will never completely intermingle as a vaulted consensus that will satisfy everybody in an oneness appreciation; consequently, everybody ends up crazy, judged by someone just because you are different. Poetry, going forward, delights with pleasure intertwining the profundity of living deducted in crazy and humor to even in the philosophical. Spring sprang; summer sizzled; autumn fell; and winter froze; these allowed rain falls, whereas grass grew; then, allowed the heat of the day to cause the flowers to blossom; allowed the leaves to fall as done in the once-a-year cycle expectancy; allowed snow to peak the mountains; inevitably, allowed the full circle return back to the spring's beginning to ever evolve, evolve, and evolve.

Notes: Heim, D. (2003). A joking matter. Christian Century, 120(16), 7.

Chapter I

[Family, Friends, Enemies, Haters, and Lovers]

Kinfolks

Comedy and funnies are always at the Kinfolks' gathering.
Uncle Ted barbecuing on the barbecue grill,
Grandpa is in his rocking chair, just a snoring.
The idea of being home is really the only thrill.

Reminiscing over forgotten trends,
It is here that the half will never be told.
Fights between the lovers and the friends,
These signify that somewhere a piece or two were sold.

Was it Ms. Pretty; who is only here for the show?
Beware, the gloves are off, and everything goes.
There is no time to practice for the slow.
At the end of the day, everybody snores.

Monkie & Punkie are both having a fabulous time.
Kinfolks are tripping and taking a sip.
Cool-aide made of beer, whiskey, and wine.
At the Kinfolks gathering, even the preacher slips and nips.

The Crazy Thing About Poetry Juxtaposed Life

Poetry tells no lies; people lie. Poetry only adorns the fancy of the believer that's within the self. In a similar context, money does not buy happiness. It is also true that poetry does not guarantee any one-way route of the emotion; just like money, it can allow you to be in a beautiful place; if, you so decide to be there. The crazy thing about poetry is the same with philosophy; there is no end to the madness. The more one thinks outside the box, the more in the box the one is contained of structure. This is even as to time; we do not get it all instantaneously. There is a stretch to everything; even, the newborn is of a nine-month ordeal. Think about how populated the world would be if a dime went into a machine and out walked a child. From the organs of the organism comes the orgasm that contains the germ, which is life. In this regards, the human species cannot claim superiority of the lower nature primates. We are just doing it too or— just maybe a few!

Money Love

The girl said, "my name is Jill."
Asked, "Did I hear you say, Bill?"
Would you like a sample of my fresh water?
You know that a drink will cost you; at least, a quarter.
The best deal in town and it's a steal!

Why hold on to all that money; you cannot take it with you?

So help a gal out, and give me a dollar or two.
Like the others, I too think you are, really swell;
Moreover, there is no one here to tell.
And, let me show you how to forget about Sue.

Give it up, and hurry here in my love joy.
You are, definitely, no little boy.
Boys play, and you know what to do.
Whereas, boys are dumb, and have no clue.
So, don't try and play me like some little toy.

Have you heard of the dance called the pony?
With what I got, I make you love me like bees making honey.
I am the teacher, and my classroom is not for the slow.
So, hurry on here and get in this boat and row.
The motion of the ocean will make you forget about money.

<u>Uncannily Clever</u>

To a large extent, I believe that we are byproducts of our own imaginative re-engineering. Philosophically and poetically, we make for ourselves a great comedy. Emotional wackos, of theme modification, in the increased

"No, *you* back off! I was here before you!"

time valued self-defining; there is no end to our foolishness. So, what did come first, "The chicken or the egg?" Our response to reasoning is all the more bizarre. As for being out of the ordinary and strange, which peripheries on the likelihood of the crazy—if there were ever an inner inspection of the real re-engineered production of who we are— what or who would you be? Poetic and Crazy!

The Next Crazy Thing

The next crazy thing is that some philosophies, even dumbfounds the philosopher as well as others in the reading thereof. The philosopher does not think, or should not think, that he spewed outside the box a perspective on the first crazy unheard in the now elevating himself to a oneness dimension. Aristotle, Plato, Kant, James and others—in essence— knew no more than the others. If they knew more, the-all would have transcended the defying wretchedness finality of death. These crazy philosophical things coming from a philosopher can be anything from a pin drop to the pleasure of the best sex ever; yet, the climax of knowing is only the initial part. It is eaten up like the "Cha-Cha placed in black eye peas of a country recipe" that is unfamiliar, to even, the average cook in the category of cooking would be to some the next crazy thing. In the stretching to everything, the widening rarely splits; however, there is the nine-month ordeal, which might beg to differ. From the organs of the organism comes the orgasm, it is this crazy philosophical pleasure that continues the germination process in the essence of living. The lofty filters down create the next crazy thing to ebb fitting the whole of ecstasy.   Affixed to all is the humor, philosophy, and poetry adorning the fancy of open awaiting the next crazy thing.

The Almost Perfect

Crazy things unfold all the time,
And, it is not always a crime.
How cares that you miss a line in a rhyme?
With friends, we all put on, the more pretending not to be.
It is not only me; from under the mask, the rest I see.

If only I controlled, I would be a great boss.
If you missed anything, I would be sad over the loss?
Everyone understands that friendship comes with a cost.
Perfection is standing alone and lonely.
The craziness inside begins to wonder, "Am I the only?"

The time put in loving makes for friendship that most hide,
Unfolding true friendship is never on the one side.
The more I strive, the more friends abide.
Perfect is time tried?

9

The excellency of friends is never full of pride.

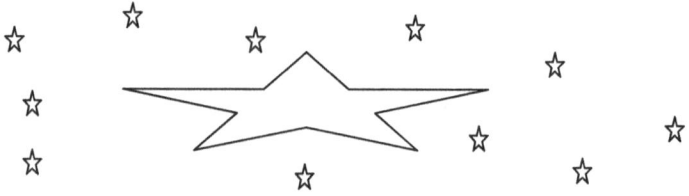

A Friend's Smile

Friendship and a smile complement every union.
These are cherished in a warming embrace.
Understanding removes friction and fiction.
It is here that endearment simplifies the case.

Friends ever so dear go out of the way to say hi!
Life's bonds daily grow stronger,
Friends are more than gold; this is no lie.
Even extends living life a little longer.

Friends and a smile create a great tie.
Together there is a seemingly magic glow.
This replaces every dull sigh.

Allows the travel of the day is moved in a beautiful flow.

At the end of the day, all is sweet and jolly.
Off to the happy hour, whereas, we enjoy this fruitful lifestyle,
With Sunday grace forgiving all of the folly.
Thanks, even now, it is of another friend's smile.

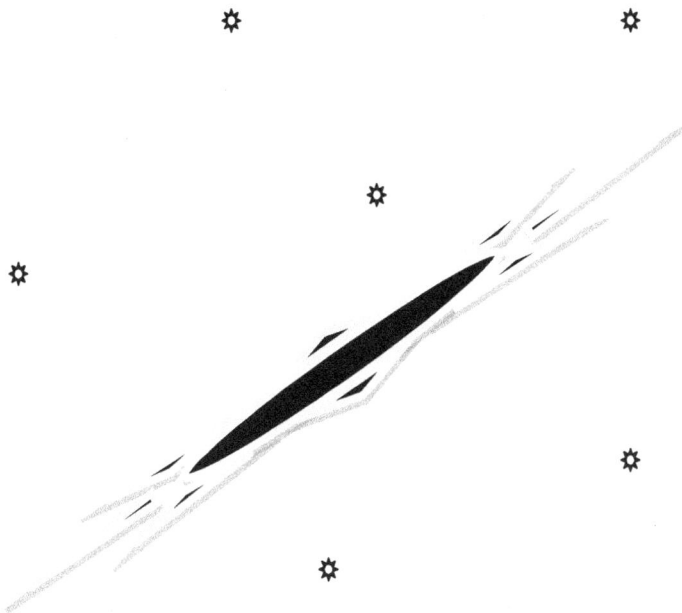

The Ecstasy of Love's Thrill

Love is not the voice of hearsay,
A cheap thrill that is passe.
Love takes a quick trip for fun in Thailand.
With a dollar in hand, who needs a plan?
Granted, it did not come to stay.

Love's thrill is the ecstasy of two.
Before it happened, we knew.
The look in the eyes told all,
Love in the autumn warms the chill of fall.
O how beautiful love grew.

Love's Thrill is its pleasure.
Ecstasy is the final measure.
It is the joy inside of Joy.
This causes one to shout, "O' girl — O'boy!"
Coming together is the greatest treasure.

Finally, in the real, we'll no longer slip, slide, or steal,
In the now, we know how the others feel.
Not willing to reach further, we settled on this as being the best.
As we say to others, "you can have the rest!"
Finally, I have love's thrill, and it is real.

The Wait for Love

Waiting can present a relaxation, the eyes closed, dreaming prior to the rigor of an obligation in an incoming affair of love. We lose ourselves in the time of desire. Despite the much that is lost in the process of waiting?

Everything seems to get lost in time, even I and then the us, time seems to be some kind of enemy. It is the stop of the comings as we go into the complement of the exploitation. Ready or not, let it come!

Humor: Last night I saw a rat chasing a cat; caught the cat, and was rewarded with a peanut. The mouse woke up the next morning with an allergic reaction. He went to the doctor. The Doctor asked, "What happened last night?" The rat responded, "Either the cat that I ate or that darn Peanut that got stuck in my mouth!" "Well, said the Doc, It is my time, now, to do the sticking— bend over!"

←──────────────────────────────────────→

Blind Love

When, where, and why are the questions.
Of all the chatting, there was but one notated.

Bizarre as it may seem; I am stunned for words.
I say, "Shame on all those wordy nerds."

Do-DI, Do –Day is the essence of the note.
You know—like up the creek without a paddle in a boat.

So— I ask, "Is there another quote?"
On the water, "Do you know how to float?"

The memo said, "It will be tomorrow."
From my brother, a tux I will borrow.

The boss is getting married.
I thought his girlfriend had a miscarriage?

Why, does this—to you—matter?
It is about money on a silver platter.

No longer can he say, "This in mine!"
There may be something in this love is blind.

LOVE'S OPPOSITES

IT IS NOT ALWAYS JUST BOY AND GIRL.
APPLE AND ORANGE ARE BOTH FRUITS; PETALS CURL.
SPIDERMAN AND SUPERMAN BOTH FLIES.
THEY TOO WANT A LOVE THAT WILL NEVER DIE.
HOWEVER, YOU HAVE TO BE A GOOD ONE-LEGGED SQUIRREL.

SUPER HEROES, ARE YOU A FAN,
CLINGING TO THE WEB IN HAND?
MOST HAVE A QUEST TO FLY.
EVEN, BIRDS, OCCASIONALLY, FALL FROM THE SKY.
IF THIS IS YOU, GET READY TO LAND.

STAYING ON THE GROUND SOUNDS LIKE A PLAN.
TO THE BEACH, LET'S PLAY IN THE SAND.
MY LOVE IS NEVER A JOKE.
ARE YOU READY TO ELOPE?
MY LEG NEEDS NO RUBBER BAND.

LOVE IS FOR BOTH THE SHORT AND TALL,
LIKE DOMINOES —WATCH THEM ALL FALL.
OR LIKE A BIRD IN THE AIR—JUST GOING WITH THE FLOW,
ALWAYS WATCHING AND LOOKING BELOW.
AS I LAY LOW, I AM WAITING THE NEXT TELEPHONE CALL.

The Lame Pickup

At the bar, the guy approaches two beautiful gals.

Player says, "It has been a long time since I saw you!"

The girl, in eye contact said, "O.K.!"

The player to bartender said, "Drinks for these two!"

The player asked, "May I sit down?"

The pretty girl said, "I am Ms. Knight,

And, what is your name."

The player said, "You know—Mr. All-Right!"

Ms. Knight said to her girlfriend, "Meet Mr. All-Rright!"

With hand extended, she said, "Hello, I am Ms. Tight!"

Mr. All-Right, I hope that we will not have to fight.

The player said, "I see that you are bright."

Not at all, this is my first time, and I here for a good time.

The two playing gals ended up as high as a Georgia Pine.

Mr. All-Right came up empty without a dime.

Without Mr. All-Right, the Gals went home feeling mighty fine.

Smiling Faces

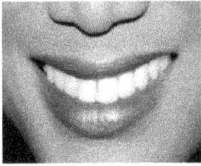

Poetry is not a person; however, poetry with us is always along for the ride in the providential gliding above the prey with a puzzling, smiling face. Is this a smile of an enemy, a friend, or a lover? All we can say, "Pretty beautiful teeth!" Is the eagle a friend or foe gliding through the blistering air current on a hot summer's day probing to feed his family. To the prey, the eagle is an enemy. The look upon the smile can we be sure—power over the powerless? On the other hand, this could be the friend's invitation. Alternatively, this can be the black willow's terminus as a terminal finality. Poetically, this can be a smile expressing, the euphemism of the pristine, with only a different kind of approval and endearment. Nonetheless, Poetry has a way of balancing the virtuous to an accepting legitimacy.

"Can you believe it, said Santa; this building has no chimney on the Jewish Christmas in November—

Didn't you know?"

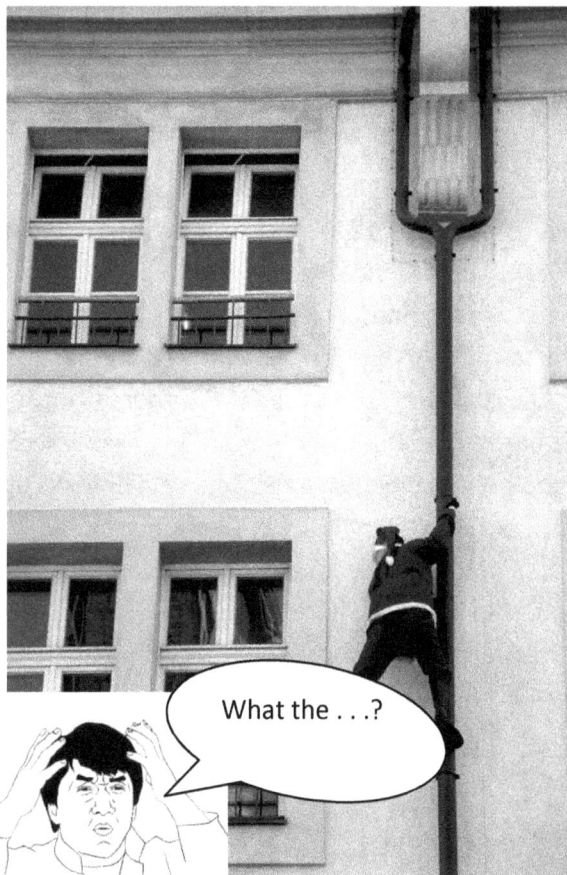

Chapter II

CRAZY TIMES

Remembering back, a friend and a friend began to replicate

events crazy and laughable as to relationships and the wacky. The events were of the poetic and wild. "Many of these events, said a friend to a friend, You know have to be on the quiet, hushed Q-T. As you know, Mama has

big ears, and she does not play, and I am not the one
wanting to pay as I lay, do your hear me Missay?"

<u>The Snake's Head</u>

Mama said, "If you take him home, he will bite.
Remember, you cannot tame all natures!
Snake eyes—like all eyes—sparkle in the light.
Snakes have to respect for anyone's culture.

With precision, you win stomping the snake's head.
Up to no good, he lays not on the ground.
The brave die and lay in coffins the same as cowards, dead!
To the snake, you are no more than a clown.

He is of powers to make you give up.
To the which, he will possess if you dare.
It is a bitter pill and drink from a dirty cup.
The snake never plays fair.

A snake is a demon along to catch a ride home.
Be careful, keep your head, and don't get robbed
As a thief, the snake steals honey from the honeycomb,
Off on the ground, he looks for his next victim and job.

Don't be fooled, a snake is not a play toy.
Tell me, have you seen a snake led?
Snakes of any kind do not make a good choirboy,
Best advice, shot the snake in the head, or you is dead.

Skydiver

Coming from school, I turned onto a gravel road.

My ride was carrying a heavy load.

I saw a girl fall from the sky.

Some girls glide and slide, but skydiver can fly,

Landed in a ditch like a toad.

On feet, she took off running like a jackrabbit.

Sitting still was not one of her habits.

The story of Skydiver for a week made for much fun,

Some say that later Skydiver became a nun.

Much like a rabbit, she daily eats cabbage.

No longer jumping and flipping to a hop,

Seminary, I understand, was her next stop.

Tweet lei door, or tweet Lee dumb,

Skydiver hits the door was not dumb suffered no harm.

I thought nuns loved nonstop.

Hole in the Wall

Do say, "Every one horse town has one."

At Hole in the Wall is where the blues won.

It's Rocking and Rolling to Johnnie Taylor,

A whisper to the other gal; "I'll see you later."

You know, the blues make one, a crazy son-of-a-gun.

Everyone out on the dance floor, doing the dog,

On the dance floor, bumping and Humping like a frog.

At the Hole in the Wall, here, everybody knows,

They all slip and slide gliding on one's toes.

For sure, the Hole in the Wall is not the synagogue.

Many a girls have been spun around like a dime,

As a player shouts, "Bartender one more round."

The Bartender retorts, "Are you sure you can afford."

As Johnnie Taylor says,

"I have two dollars: one for the jukebox and one for the road."

Got what I want, and I am feeling mighty fine.

Home first, as I take care of Ms. Sleepy.

All the while thinking about Ms. later, that's creepy.

Two in one night is my real plan.

I forgot to tell you, "They call me 'Batman'"

The Hole in the Wall is the place for the "Sneaky!"

If, you want to know more;

Lovers do not sleep and snore.

I Looked at Ms. Sleepy as I hit the door.

Left her still there on the floor!

If she awake, the note says, "I went to the store."

Hello, Ms. Later, I hope I am not too late.

I see you saved this for me, what a plate!

"Sit down, she said, get comfortable and eat."

It was on, as she sat me in my favorite seat.

She said to me, "you are my only special date."

Afterward, I said, "I know, Ms. Later,

And I must say you are one hot potato!"

I will see you tomorrow, at the Hole in the Wall.

alligator gumbo

If not, you know that I will call?

"See you later alligator!"

<u>What is the Poetic?</u>

The life of poetry and the love of poetry are larger than any one person. The expressions of living poetry and loving poetry are about a two— intermingled with vital similarities to being almost one. It is the calmness and the coziness of the two that wraps the heart in the delivery of satisfaction with the pumping up and out joy in the midst of clamor and emotions. The two (life and love) draws together an irresistible enticement that bundles joy beyond the expression of words. Poetry's life and poetry's love get trapped in the mind travels toward the novel's possibility that charms the chic luxury of the adorned. Poetic life is the simplistic living of every individual. Poetic love is of its audience on the voyage for those that are full of life and is living it to the fullest. In a joyful sense, this makes the poetic little crazy, wouldn't you say?

<u>Crazy Love</u>

I heard a long time ago, "Two with a gun is no fun!"

This means someone should have sense enough to run.

However, my gun is a gun of the squirrel.

Whereas, two of a kind creates a null and is dull.

Just bumping heads, no way to get anything done!

Bay-bee, I am just a three-legged squirrel looking for a nut.

So put away your toy—and, let's do "The What."

Do you hear me, Ms. Fine?

I'm not here to dine, but I'll take a glass of wine.

Don't shoot when I tell you that, "You have a pretty butt!"

Your Gun may be fun, but mine is so much better.

Get rid of that useless toy, and take off all that leather.

Let play another game as I groove you.

I have the gun, and there is no need for two.

There's nothing more beautiful than two coming together.

Trust me, mine is the new thrill of Crazy.

Come on! What's more, I want you to stop being lazy.

I have a loaded shotgun, and my thrill is real.

Even puking, I can't see you losing your sex appeal.

Already, you have my head spinning like a daisy.

My love toy and your love joy are a great mix.

Riding my cowboy's pony is your next lick.

A salad, ranch dressing, and no meat are for Crazy lovers,

With a gun, a horse, and oysters are best undercover.

"So long boy, I am not your next trick!"

<u>What's Real?</u>

Love is like the up and down game of the stock market.

Reality, one should not put all eggs in one basket.

Like stock, who know when love will fall?

From the best evidence, love and the stock market can take all,

Being broke is as being dead in a casket.

So tell me, if you know, what's real?

Is buying life insurance a good deal?

What I want to know, where can I buy forever insurance?

We just insure your life; living is never an assurance.

I guess this is how it is in the game called, steal.

Today, even, the spiritual is for sale,

Today, even, some guys are named Gail.

Telling everyone to repent or they are going to hell,

With all the hoopla, I'll be better off with Jezebel.

No one, any longer, cares anything about blackmail.

Which one is real, the stock market, insurance, or the spiritual?

Got it! All are real when you are looking for a miracle.

In the end, it is all about what and whom you know.

The only requirement is that you have some doe.

Keeping it real, it's not my fault that I sound a little cynical.

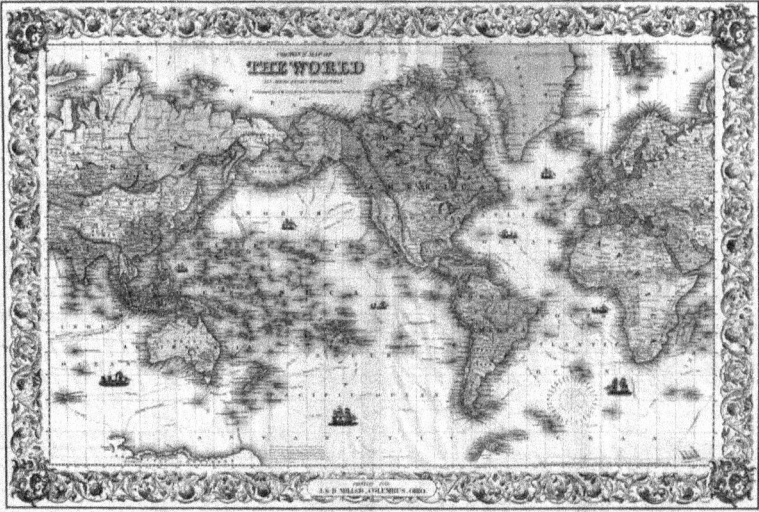

Chapter III

Crazy Disinformation

Columbus Discovered America

The American history of Christopher Columbus is all a lie in three documented regards:

(1) Columbus did not prove the world was round;

(2) Columbus never set foot on North America's shores; and

(3) Columbus massacred many inhabitants of the Caribbean. (Strauss, 2013).

Liars' Piece

We discovered America, and we created the Indian people.

However, we could not give the names like, Christopher or Peter.

They kept demanding soap and hope.

Therefore, we had no choice but to give them dope.

They reject slavery, and they turned us into haters.

These things you need to know to keep your sanity.

Serving their God made the Indians sacrilege.

They thought they owned land that was mine.

Like it or not, Indians were behind the times.

As slaves, we would have given them many work privileges.

I told the Indians I cut down the cherry tree; "I cannot tell a lie!"

However, someone else stole the cherries needed for the pie?

You know; I am the president; my last name is Washington.

I am the first and the only honest "Charlatan!"

What is more, this is just a man wearing a necktie.

Furthermore, "I did not sleep with that woman!"

Nonetheless, Viagra has been my daily vitamin.

Marilyn too was under a few presidents.

Neither of them were dissidents.

CIALIS too can be a good daily vitamin regimen.

"I am not a Crook!" I am as honest as Lincoln.

The only difference is I was not an African.

The fact is, my telephone line got crossed with Jimmy's.

It was that darn Congress that refused to give me just one penny.

Impeached me! At breakfast, this made me throw up my bacon.

My ancestors too have a connection all the way back to Africa.

I have always been faithful to the swastika,

My face says, "humps and bumps.

I played the race card, and the money is my trump.

Have you never read the books called the Britannica?

The Philosophy in Crazy Disinformation

Visually, crazy disinformation is a perceived acuity that tingle the receptors in the mind of those doing the interpreting. Notwithstanding, the pictorial is untrustworthy. The misplaced is in a faint nonrepresentational notion of time and space.

The inner rim of disinformation bamboozles swindling to a magnetization trapping the beguiled. Herein, the imagery's perspicacity is fogged with lies, which creates impracticable tangible elucidated particulars. The quotidian imagery—of the ordinary everyday kinds—flares as a newly

contained wildfire of fiery with varying pockets of misleading reactionaries (e.g., the demagogue of politics that plays on the emotions, passions, and prejudices of would-be voters). The philosophy of the visual is the strenuous sting of the serpent's ploy to bewilder and exploit for selfish gain. How far can the imagination be stretched? Is beauty in eyes of the beholder? The stretched cause and effect of imagery's actions — analyzing history— have produced pockets of our societies to strike death blows into the heart of humanity. The notion that one group of humans is inferior to another is the foundation of enslavement. The philosophy in the crazy is in the

heart of deceit that hates, filled with bigotry that impoverishes, and robs the mind of fruitfulness.

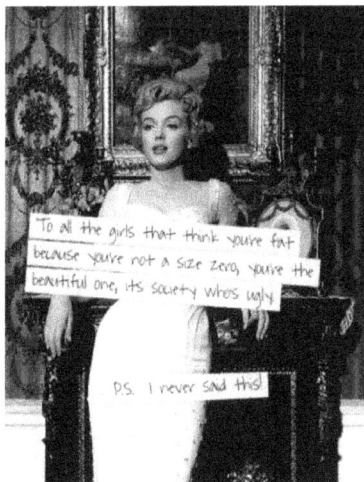

The interpreted beauty is too of the mind that is convoluted by the crazies, and all sorts of disinformation to the receiver thereof. Someone said the other day, "That darn Hollywood can take a pig, dress her up, and tell you she is the new beauty queen of the world." Hello, Ms. Pretty! To that, we will accept, such as truly authentic, and we will not ask how and why." Just imagine what's to come! Aside from the contemptuous, life is exciting— isn't it?

★

End of War

Can the voice of a president over the bow be a fabrication,

Filled with lies, particulars and falsifications?

The announcement seemed sound with no explication,

Became the greatest voice of pacification.

O how, half-truths become the great mystery.

To even, the events that reshape History.

Bush-Washed returned in a mighty fiery.

This begs for the eventual coming of Hillary.

War's Ending is an enemy of an enemy is a friend.

To whom can you depend on and defend?

A trillion dollars in the account of the "misspend,"

Of course, such amount is hard to comprehend.

O', we were never in a war; this was just a conflict.

36

Could this, too, be one of the Devil greatest tricks?

Despite the fact, we should not appear overly strict.

War's Ending is just right for a shoe or a brick.

Listening, did you miss the concept that money must flow?

If one thinks otherwise, you are— sure slow!

This is the same sniffing blow and selling the snow.

You know! The double talk of the great whore.

Who says she lied, cheat, steal, and kills?

Off the top, her money till has to be filled,

Dope is not the pharmaceutical bottle of pills.

War's ending, conflict or not, there are no thrills.

The Magical Sleight of Hand

I caught a glimpse of a man with no arms the other day.

He stood on the corners, and in a Can—drivers they pay.

Seeing no traffic, the money went into the man's pocket.

No hands, the money deposited as fast as a rocket.

I saw this, just today, what else do you want me to say?

The most likely place for the hand is on an arm.

Therefore, you saw no arm; indeed, the man cannot farm.

Here is a dollar or two that makes me feel better.

Despite I have had a bad day in expected turbulent weather.

I paid and hurried home to a bottle of rum.

I know that seem a bit crazy,

However, it also shows that I am not lazy.

With a sleight of hand, I tried to take some out.

My hands somehow got cut, made me shout,

This started me thinking about "Driving Miss Daisy."

Conclusion, impairment does not always mean handicap.

Handicap or not, it is never good taking the rap.

    With a need to Grow an arm or two for just the folding.

    It is a different card, if you bet, as to what I am holding.

    Beware, the magical sleight of hand is my man, Chap.

The Magic of Love

Magic is of a oneness dynamic, which is lively whether on the stage or in the bosom of the age old act called love. Now for such come the inexplicable non-reasoning thriller. It is the joie-de-vivre (vibrancy) from the magic that creates an effervescence that can alter and reshuffle the sited schedule of a gorilla. Here, it is for a two-step that allows the moon to walk out of a hat like a rabbit that we see— or, maybe not! Then begs the question, is this, an angel or the devil in disguise? Regardless, the heart begins to beat like an Indian drum, tummy tom tummy-ing around a camp fire. This is not the same illness of the textbook variety with bodily equilibrium going around to sizzle the heart. Could there be a higher order in magic directed to this seeming reality? Even when eyes are shut and wired tight, there is the everything that seems bright as day. The magic of love's causation sprouts and springs linked-in of the heart to the kingdom called Neverland. Despite the fly away effect, feet are firmly placed back on the ground after the moon walk and

the dance of brake. These bubble everything in the magical tale of two cities with love being in-between of the dinner and the movie.

Notes

(1) One of the greatest **Speech,** as a notation, ever:

During my lifetime, I have dedicated myself to this struggle of the African people. I have fought against white domination, and I have fought against black domination. I have cherished the ideal of a democratic and free society in which all persons live together in harmony and with equal opportunities. It is an ideal that I hope to live for and to achieve. However, if needs be, it is an ideal for which I am prepared to die~Nelson Mandela.

(2) Strauss, V. (2013). Christopher Columbus: 3 things you think he did that he did not. Retrieved from The Washington Post:http://www.washingtonpost.com/blogs/answer-

Crazy!

Chapter IV

Crazy "P's"

"P" of poetry gets us started after the craziness of the "I" as [in] an interpretive applied to each stanza. Never start with [and]; and, but, all the while you were under the impression that all "P's" belonged to Paul; even, the pussycat  gets a "P!" The crazies of craziness are to the "P's" in/of the word published. . .. "Crazy, as one said, makes and mixes for what crazy does!"   Into the door, here steps, for starters, "P" Diddy's billions.

Unraveling the mystery of the poetic forever is in the intoxication that senses a journey to wonderland; the "P" that pleases almost resurrects "**Topac** and **M. J.**" in the lost of self-control. Did you say "P" is for pill? Hello Dr. Feelgood! Call who? Bill Cosby does not have a "P" in his name. O' I got you, " IN THE 'P!'" It's the crazy "P's" all around the drama. Does this make sense, or am I just crazy? *C-by the P-her sold a P-l to the P-r-ute that gave C-by some P –sy for a P-l. Miss P-r-ute is now lying to the P-ice because they are broke trying to get P-ad from the P –licity. They are hoping for some type of P-y form C-By the P-her; so that, they can find another P-her to get more P-ls because there P-sy is old, and they no longer can get P-ls by selling their old ass P-sy.* I told you— **Crazy "P!"** By the just *Poetic and Crazy*, I am just thinking out loud in the first person; I don't know anything; plus, I might be a little touched!   It looks like fine wine to me; although, I am not so sure—"Suck or Sip?" I may deal with the "S's" at some other point; just thinking, the "S" does seem to sound a little more exciting than the "P!"

You do know that "P" really stands for pig, like piggy-bank. It's all in the bank; the Pig is on top. Got the View?

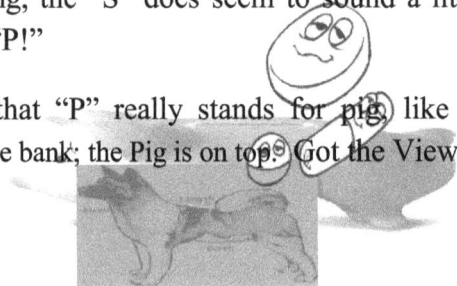

Dick and Crazy Peter

In the ward of the schizophrenics, Dick begins to talk with Peter.
Dick said to Peter, "You know we are one, but I am sweeter."
Peter retorted, "Who cares, you are still a prick!"
Peter went on asking, "When last, have you had a good Lick?"
"I know," says Dick, "Then too, you are bee eater!"

"Dick, I have a new name for you—Willie!"
"Peter, what's on your head, a rubber cap?—you look so silly!"
Peter said, "It is better to look silly than to be dripping wet."
Dick said, "You won't get pregnant, but you might sweat!"
"Forget you," said Peter, "I have a date with an African Lily.

"I dress up," said Peter, "To keep from messing UP!"
Dick said angrily, "You are still a chump!"
Peter said to Dick, "You are nothing but a snake!"
Dick replied, "It's better to be a snake than a fake."
Peter laughed, "At least I know how to hump!"

Did Someone Say
Hump?

Crazy Poetry in People

Poetry is just a hitchhiker along for a free ride through the "P's" of calm places. In the **P**rojects of the hood, the show is ever evident, contrary to the well-to-do **P**eople-hoods. Poetry visit the home of a well-to-do **P**rotected and ran away mad as a did-a-bug; caught a ride with the **P**itch-folk gardener, and learned Mexicana along the way. Got dropped off in the

45

hood, caught a ride with the **P**reacher—learned how gives blessing to the will to be blessed. Poetry met a **P**oliceman learned how to be **P**olite and a new song, "Shot'em b'fore they run now!" Moved out and caught a ride with a **P**rostitute and learned how to lie. Poetry said to self, "Oh, what a wonderful day, I will ride again tomorrow, maybe on a **P**ony this time, off into the new sunset for another **P**leasurable **P**iece. . . LOL!!!" People should be just **P**eople **P**leasing **P**leasure. Who knows; the next time it might be you who get **P**aid!

Crazy "P"leasing Woman

In the Beginning, she was the pleasure of life.
After removing the rib, she kept the piercing knife.
In a stable position, she has finally arrived.
And, with persuasion is how she thrives.

In a man's place, do you really think you know a woman?
If she says **fine**, this means that you need to shut-up, man.
There is nothing left to say; she is right, and has won the argument.
Saying more is to add fuel to a burnt out fire and bad judgment.

If she says, please give me **10 minutes** to dress, this means 1 hour.
The pleasure, in fantasy, is at least 30 minutes alone in the shower.
The rest is spent between dressing and prepping.
If the prep is right, you can stop praying..

And, if she comes out **saying nothing**, you get on your "P" and "Q!"
"P" is to say please, "Q" is to be quiet with very cautious questions.

? Knowing all, this could be the eye before the storm.
And, you could catch hell before you get home.

Her day has already been made, if she says to you, "**Go Ahead**,"
This is not some kind of **permission**; you could end up "Dead!"
The words of a woman say, "Go Ahead" is more of a dare.
One wrong word or wrong move, the fire can easily flare.

The "Huh" of a loud sigh from a woman sees you as an idiot,
And to her, your head looks like a giant size peanut.
As she wonders about a nut, she thinks she is just wasting her time.
So, she races home and grabs two bottles of wine.

Therefore, in the end, pleasing a woman is about her pleasure.
It's about something she got that you cannot measure.
Of all the good of the world, this is what she mostly treasures.
Man, believe me when I tell you, It is never about your plethora.

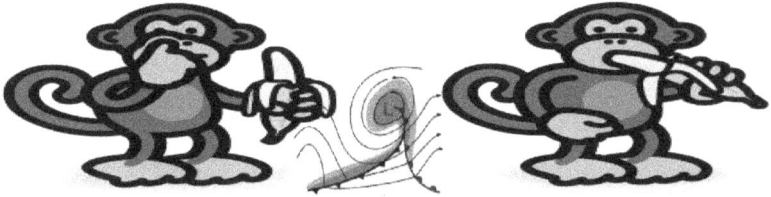

Guilty Pleasures

The Crazy Pleasure of Pleasures

The craziness of pleasures has never known a stable sensation.
From creation, the world has been heading toward cremation.
Can we say that both are the same in life and death?
Or, do we say, it is in just the pulsation of each breath?
At the end of each ecstasy, there is always another temptation.

Someone just inserted the pleasure of increased population.
Many are in a mad rush to the altar of jubilation.
The choice of pleasure is filled with the cost of pain.
These make two become one in some crazy game called "gain."
So that everyone is comfortable with our explanation.

This is the way it has been for generation after generation.
Some say, this sucks and let's march in next demonstration,
Protesting the status quo relating to pleasure's crime.
It's a mad rush home for a little more downtime.
The pleasure of demonstrating opens a door for cohabitation.

Bedfellows and foes come together for sexual affirmation.
Pleasure wins again receiving a might climatic confirmation.
It's crazy and beyond means; all is insanity.
And, pressed for love increased the satisfied intensity.

48

With pleasures opening, pleasure receives a forceful, pleasing infiltration.

The Crazy Pop Top

A hot bubble-bath and a glass of wine is a party.
The incoming of mate makes the party jovial and hearty.

We popped another cork, and bubbles burst.
Is loving some momentary curse?
It feels so good or is it the pop of the cork that has me jolly?

Crazy Politics

The poetry of politics is of a truth with each politician lying without being a liar. In crazy politics, you lie, not because you liar, but because the public do not like you anymore; therefore, and now, you have to lie the more, but to no avail. If the public like you, you can keep on lying, and your lies are not lies although you are lying. *"A Lie of an enemy about an enemy is the truth with none being friends."*~ Sherman Jones.

This is the craziness of the status quo; whereby, the politicians' actions, definitions, and poem lines are not the same are yours under the rules in the consequential. I can cross-dress—just thinking out loud— wearing women panties, shoes, dresses, wigs, and lipstick, but I am not a homosexual because I have a wife, children, and strong connections. **Sidebar:** *I have an Empire State Building that you can buy for a million dollars. If you rush it to me by tomorrow, I guarantee you it will fit in your backyard in Alaska overlooking Moscow.*

Therefore, the lie you see is not a lie because I am different from you, and the rules for me are different. I am ten (10) feet tall. I wear an eighteen (18) inch shoe. I ride around town in a Mini Bug with an elephant in the trunk. I must tell you that politics are not for sale. This is why the elephant would not let the mule get in my Mini Bug trunk and come along. Trust me, I will never tell you a lie! Drop over for dinner, I am at the "Brothers' House," its duck soup warmed over a time or two; trust me, you will love it. If you hate two, you will love three. It's just an arrow in the back. Stop your

whining! I could have shot two. Can't we all just get along?
The Crazy "P" of politics, Trust Me!

Happy Turkey Day Prize

Can you hear the turkeys in wood talking?

Tomorrow is Happy Turkey day.

You better keep on walking.

Or, on the table, you will lay.

Man, I have not had a chance to get in shape.

Don't worry, they will still dress you.

Hurry, we might still be able to escape.

Or, they will butcher you

Why is it that they call this Happy Turkey Day?

I do not know; they did not check with me.

I guess they think we dodging bullets are our play.

Oh, that makes sense, and now I see.

Hurry, here comes the convoy.

With guns, they hunt their prey.

Like an invading army ready to destroy.

Have a Happy Turkey Day!

Chapter V

Mom
My ex Lolcats Starbucks
Eminem Lady Gaga
Fail xkcd Fashion
YouTube Owned
OMG Britney
Barbie Winning
Rhianna
Lying
Regret
Funny
Fear
Google
Planning Twitter
Dreams Lust Babies
Daydreams Facebook
Pride Porn
Horror Guilt Hope
Work
More porn

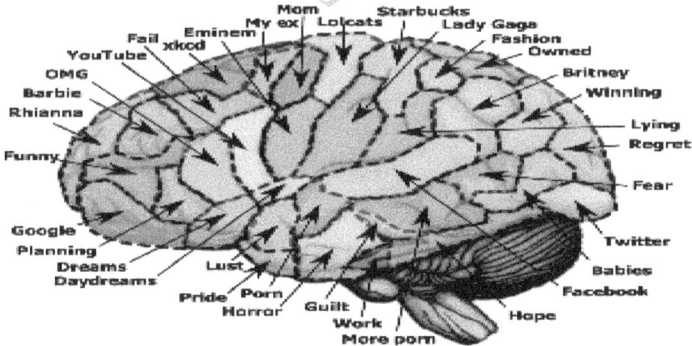

Crazy Poetic Philosophy

The brain lives in infinity seeking to know nothing, but houses all of the senses' abilities to share—of its own self has nothing to share. The privilege to be crazy is not without cost. It de-energizes the phenomena of the spongy mask triangulation to the senses' input down to a stumbling drunkard ant.

Imagine
Forever

However, we think we know; all the while, the brain knows otherwise— if the brain knows anything. This is the great

53

complexity of having a brain; knowing your mind knows nothing. However, we are not to allow this to confuse us because the brain is a tool; the mechanism does all our dirty work. If the brain knew or had the ability to do anything, the brain would always be knocking the living socks off of us. As time passes, the brain's functionality began depreciating the cherished stops serving our buffoonish dictates.

Moon Philosophy

I landed somewhere in the far away, nothing but rocks and sand.

I knew I had made it; the day was hot and night dark over the land.

It was the land of the home that this moon created a thirst.

After a brief stay in this moon's philosophy, they shot me back to first.

Who was I to question the bright lights, cameras, and the shaking of the hands?

No Question Philosophy

In a world of obscurity, the day is no longer the same as light.

Above the law, the pendulum swings, apparently no longer as right.

It is the zenith philosophy of demons' "No Questions."

The anus gases of the smelly irritants' indigestion.

The ashen night is clearly seen in the clan of Knight.

The corruptible night's clash stretch is not a novelty.

Darkness hides the pale until one sees the trees.

This is the same as seeing the bees swarming hive.

To Kill a Mockingbird's lynching is no jive.

The tree of every corner experiences a killing spree.

Hands off questioning a thousand years of malice.

She might be the queen, but for sure, she is not Alice.

She stomps the dark horse candidate riding a white horse.

Allowed the intercourse, and she asked for no divorce.

Because, up-the-road, she saw the hill as an invincible force.

55

Breaking the fraternity seems to be a barrier to the climb.

If traced back, humanity would go to jail serving time.

Thief of every kind is the crime with a world losing the victory.

The substantiations are bowled over rooted in history.

The evil of the no question philosophy is an infernal crime.

The Crazy Poetic Philosophy

The *Crazy Poetic Philosophy* of the **Whereis** about whether or not we of consciousness ever exist before the now. The travels, to and fro, are incoherent with a night in the tangibility

substantiating knowledge of the indescribable. The scientific vacuuming of this particular— consciousness before, during, and after existence— quagmires to an easy repudiation of any supposed conclusive. At the same time, any and all can contain a degree grain of probability. Crazy is when you know because this what Crazy Poetic Philosophy is all about—knowing. This is where the expressed vented—whether openly or not poetically— acknowledges the jingles in a plausibility's continuum. The craziness is of the out-of-mind that incites the rudimentary weaving an intertwine of convening platitudes fiddling an organ in-the-mind of the corporeal.

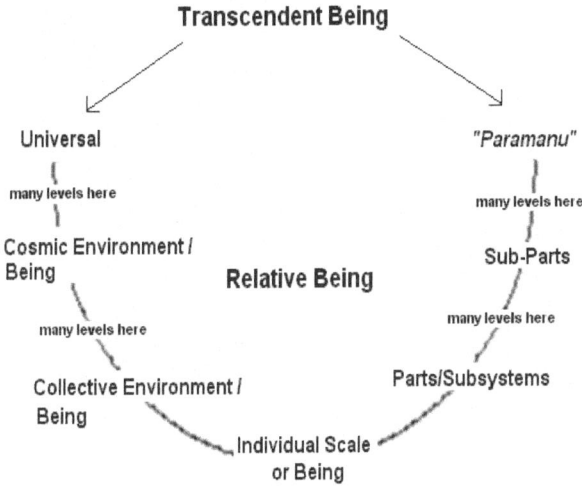

Transcendent Being

Universal   *"Paramanu"*

many levels here   many levels here

Cosmic Environment / Being   **Relative Being**   Sub-Parts

many levels here   many levels here

Collective Environment / Being   Parts/Subsystems

Individual Scale or Being

...That is by no means an attempt on my part to emphasize my manhood.

58

Chapter VI

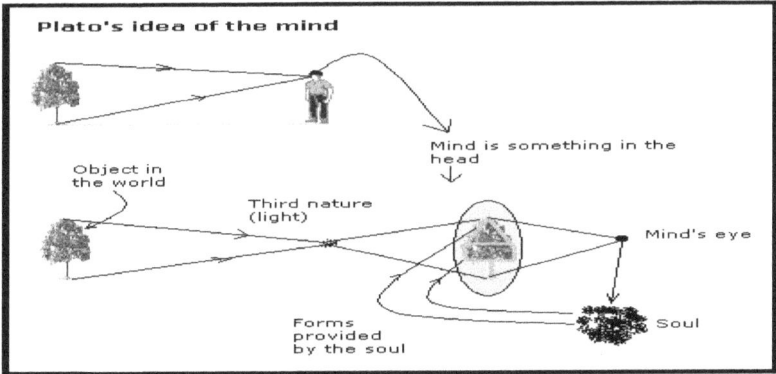

Plato's idea of the mind

Object in the world

Mind is something in the head

Third nature (light)

Mind's eye

Forms provided by the soul

Soul

The Crazy Poetic Mind's Eye

This crazy game is called **Hide and Seek**. Find me if you can! The mind's eye, in my head, has viewed an object that I think is appropriate for me to hide behind. If your mind's eye sees me, my mind's eye will respond to your voice that says, "I got you!" My mind's eye will tell me to beat you back to the base; and, maybe, I'll win the game. Furthered is this crazy game of the mind's eye; whereas, the soul, nature, and objects are all in interplay of "I got you, and I won!"

Crazy Soul Food

As if beamed from heaven into the cotton field's hood,

O brother was saved from hunger with a dish called "Soul Food!"

"What's all this excitement about, Give me some," said the Master.

Soul Food made the master procreate birthing many bastards.

The master's love of soul food caused even the pigs to get screwed.

Soul Food is a dish loved by all, from the head to the feet.

The master saw and said, "These are hog guts— o. k., I'll eat!"

After a while, the master started looking like a hog;

Thought he was eating Coon, but he was eating his dog.

Chitlins, dogs, and Mountain Oysters were the master's feast!

Soul Food went to four corners and made masters slap their Mamas,

That was a mistake, the master got hit in the head with a mama's hammer.

Mama killed the master and chicken— then said, "Finger licking- good!"

You can have your Texas barbecue. I want mama's soul food from the hood.

Believe me when I tell you, "Don't mess with mama; she is a bad Mamma-Jamma.!"

Side Bar Humor

Somewhere I hear the following:

I had a little sense.

I hung it on a fence.

The wind came along,

and I have not seen it since.

SAVING THE WORLD

It is not my fault that you don't have a gun.

Even, stupid understands the concept of run.

Salvation's cross is under the hoods' advice.

And, the fire has nothing to do with Christ!

If I am lying, dying is fun.

We mean no harm; we are just trying to save the lost.

Don't forget, we are the boss,

However, Relax, enjoy, and live in peace.

I am not trying to hit you; I am after the flea.

It, just, seems as if you are in some type of cross.

We love the same everywhere; this is just another corner!

Despite the death cries of the mourners.

Don't forget I could use the gas.

Hands up— O' I was just kicking the flea's ass.

However, watch out for the shoe— despite your honor.

Thank you, Master, for saving me is the world's cry.

In spite of the words, "You must die!"

Now, I know there will be peace all over the world.

Pi greco
in versi

In the ear, this is whispered by a nut coming squirrel.

All things are going to be as sweet as mom's apple pie.

3.14159265₃₅₈

Crazy Or is it ME?

Philosophy's clichés are crazy no matter how much sense it makes.

It is like saying to me that sugar is not necessary to bake a cake.

By the way, this is true; however, "that said," this is still crazy all the same.

A masterful play on words, this has always been the game.

As I wish no longer a part of you, I say, "Go, jump in a lake!"

How often you view pictures that just seem out of place.

Around someone's neck, there hangs a shoe lace.

To the bar to quench my thirst,

I am in a hurry to get there, but I do not want to be first.

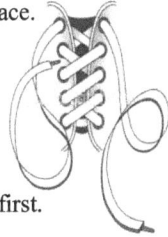

Keeping up with the Joneses has nothing to do with my running pace.

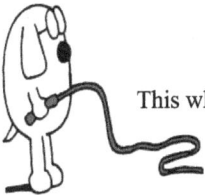

This whipping is going to hurt me more than you.

Well, let me whip you so that I know you are telling the truth.

Yesesa Master, I know what you mean.

It is the same; give me the steak, and you eat the beans.

Now, I am wiser, but I was stronger in my youth.

HERE COME THE JUDGE

From the Bench

I guess! To be humorous, one must be a little touched. "It is truly crazy," I know! Therefore, you must get a bit of a background before we hear from the judge.

Sidebar Humor:

Three young men rest in jail awaiting their day in court. One is a Caucasian; the others are a Hispanic and an African-American. Each received charges for speeding and booked. Now, it is before the bench; and- now, let us hear from the judge. The judge first asked the young Caucasian man, "How old are you?" He replied, "I am 19, your Honor!" Immediately, the judge said, "91 days in jail," slamming his hammer to the bench. Turns now to the Hispanic young man and asked, "How old are you, Mexican?" The Hispanic young man answer, "I am 18, your judge!" "81 days in jail," shouted the judge. The young black man was learning all the while as to the sentencing philosophy of the judge and said to himself, "okay!" Then the judge said, "N. . .! How old are you?" My brother shouted back at the judge and said, "Your Honor, I am only 11 years old, and I do not care how you flip it, it will still be 11!" Because of his smart arrogance, the judge said, "Correct, slammed his hammer on the bench stated further, "One year and one day in jail!" The hold court room rolled and burst a stitch laughing. The jailer still laughing took the three prisoners back to their cell and said to the African American, "See what you get for being so smart!" The African American young man replied, "I guess this is why they call it 'Just-Us!'"

<u>Old School Speaks</u>

I know that they call you, *My Boo*!

Just like a ghost, you are what the wind blew.

Thinking you are all that with some new game.

This, just, shows to the world that you are really lame.

Trick or Treat, Babe Boo, Hurry and return to the zoo!

Apparently, you do not know that *more* mean the same.

Oh, yes! It is a game; one that no man can change.

Watch out Mr. Wrong Lane, don't get hit by Lois.

I don't believe it; Superman is kissing Doris!

You two (Boo & Lane) have no game.

You better listen to *"School"* and stop being a fool.

All suckers at first seem cool!

There is no such thing as luck.

"Watch out sucker—Duck!"

Before, falling off the Barstool.

At this rate, you might not reach a ripe old age.

They look up monkeys putting them in a cage.

There, you will end up in love —hugging *"Big Buddy!"*

And, that will not be so funny.

Or worse, you can end up on the *"Front-Page!"*

Listen to *"School,"* she loves you no more than the other.

One from Boo and two from Lane go a lot further.

Like kryptonite, she will knock out "Superman?"

Batman & Robin could well do according to her plan.

Old *School* said, "Never forget— she is not your mother."

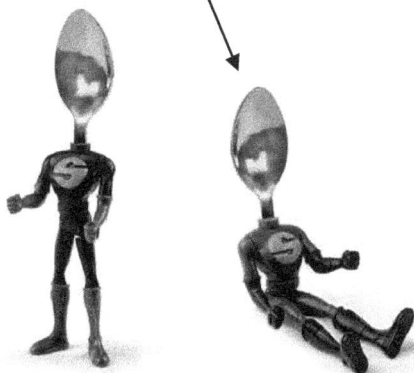

Chapter VII

Where the Rubber Meets the Road

Here is a great philosophical question!

Have you ever seen a three-legged squirrel, on a crutch, attempting to cross the freeway after seeing a Pea-nut?

HA! HA! HA!   Whatever!

The Lack of Speed in Traveling Time

The propinquity of every great work, in as a play on being, is about time. This is the moments of the evolved to the sempiternal (the lasting forever). Albeit, the "at life in the suddenness. This is the up-ness in the like of a fir tree in the midst of a forest with a boulder rock sitting in the mist. The question comes as to how did it all happen and from whence it came? All now emulate the pristine inception of the shared warmth, cooling down the once smelting boulder of the volcanic lava, which now is older than once was is not as sultry in the mystery. Time knows nothing of niceties. Regardless of mysteries surrounding the boulder's melt down that swirls in the challenging hunger of man's mind. Conceptualization can either be fast or slow depending on the point of beginning that is used in the analysis. This causes some readers to climax in the culmination with a book that is liken to the anonymity that gratifies the supplied covetousness that lust supplementary in

the accompanying intertwine. The need for more and the lack of climax within acceptable curvature. The same lack of relative time challenges the-every with both connotation and denotation amid each verse's insatiably attempting to catch up with the speed of time. The penetration opens as a subterranean hole amid each philosophical, poetic line of the intended. Despite the lack of speed, pleasure is desired or felt in the essential with the desideratum unraveling slowly in the created maturation. Suddenly, as in an abrupt stop of full, a volcanic eruption explodes in the space of time.

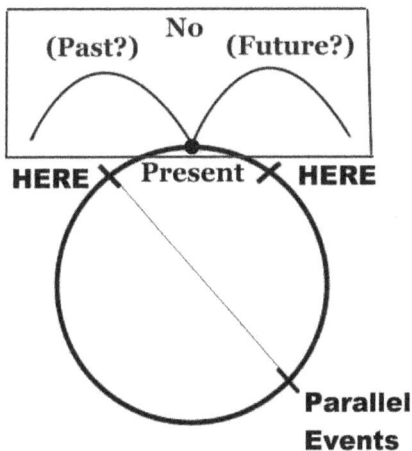

71

A New Day Dawn

My head is empty; of all, what's the source?
　I know; the beautiful song about the river and moon.
As the Stars dance, we too had fun to every course.
　Dancing, we talked about being home soon.

Before dawn, I wish upon a star in the night,
　　　Give me you love and don't be late.
　　As Cupid, my arrow will shoot the light.
　　　A candle, wine and dine, work a great date.

　　Lying and waiting continue the wish upon a star.
　This Boo might be the greatest lay!
I sure love his beautiful shinny new car.
I am going to all I can to make him stay.

It was Fire and Desire— Rick and Tina singing.
　Hello and how are you, Your "Majesty?"
My head is spinning with bells ringing.
Whenever, you can always be my bookie.

Every night fall leads us to another day.
There penetrated by the love of boldness.
The cat is caged and never again stray.
　Oh' the drunk-ness of hypnosis!

Got up the morning after, I sang hallelujah.
　He's all of that; A man of men!
Let this not be the "Tragedy of Othello!"

With all tragedies, in the end, no one wins.

The sleepy dead of night, suddenly adorns in lust.
Realizing now, the night used us as a pawn.
This is enough to make a guy or gal Curse.
At most, we say, "It's a new day dawn.

VEGAS

It's not just the dice.
There are the weddings and the rice.
I am here in the hotels with all the comforts of home.
I got married in Vegas now no longer a reason to roam.
In my pocket, there is money, and everyone is so nice.

The lights glittered, and on the streets, there are no skid marks.
The bellman is always willing to take your car to park.
Everyone is so polite at every tip.
This is by far the greatest of all road trips.

Rarely did I ever hearing dogs barking.

Security and cameras everywhere, makes one feel so safe.
A rush to the slot machine, there is this arm of a saber.
A quick pull on bandit, I got more money in my pocket.
Later in room, the marriage filled the love's socket.
Got off like a rocket and ended up chafe.

Like a wolf on a hill, barking at the moon.
Got up and back slot machine around noon.
Two and two equal four, why is it I have three.
Vegas kept one so that I would not flee.
Lost all, thought that I was immune.

TIGER ROAD

Off to the woods and the big game of the wild.

My golf game is off, so I just rest a while.

Shoot me a bear or catch me a deer.

There in no one left to question me, what have I to fear?

I forgot about the game warden, and the smile.

I might do better in Rwanda.

Of true nature, where do lions wonder?

And, elephants are friendly.

Sounds like a great place to fill the belly.

There is nothing left to ponder.

I have the balls, and this time I have the clubs.

In Rwanda, the waitresses own the pub.

I think I will give it a twirl.

Just like what I am, a silly squirrel.

To me, Monkey brains sound like the grub.

My mind is just in a whirlpool of desire.

I'll be back and will turn on the fire.

Stop hating the player, hate the game.

Not me, it's the other leg due the blame.

That turned me into a night's vampire.

A Cab Ride

With an unlock heart, I took a cab ride to dinner.

The driver was professional despite looking in the mirror.

I liked the look—so, I moved to the center.

This cabby was really a winner.

I could tell away from the cab he is a real swinger.

Down the road, in the ride, I was feeling mighty fine.

I thought to myself and said, "My time to wine and dine!"

Other than the cabbie, I might get lucky a get me a good time.

You know— one that talks sweet over a glass of wine.

Real or a lie, I really like a good line.

All the while, I could not stop thinking about cabbie.

The ride was going smoothly, and I was happy.

'Cause in an odd sort of way, cabbie reminded of pappy.

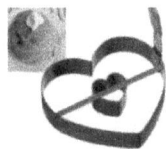

He was smooth and sweet, but not syrupy.

He was talkative, but he was not crappy.

At the restaurant, he jumps out and opens my door.

Made to feel like a queen by a cabbie that was not a bore.

I am a professional and a perfect gentleman to the core.

A man with class is always what I adore.

Pardon me, you are wrong; I am no whore!

A Riding Question

Every question relating to philosophy is a sort of ride along. I guess one can say a type of hitchhiker. In one sense or poetry can be a type of philosophy because it expresses, of sorts, the deepest and most intimate thoughts of the author. Poetry can be philosophical and at the same time be informal. The irony lays with the intended genre that paradoxes formal philosophy. It depends; in many instances, who you want to ride along with, and what you want to do after the ride. It is now the question, what's your dream car? Move over Mercedes

and let Bentley take us home. Or is it the sporty Porsche?
What's the point? A ride is a ride; who cares?   Wrong, this
cannot be because, if so, every poem would be the same without
variations and Aristotle would have the one and only speaker.
The types and styles are endless and rightly so or else we would
all die from boredom. The ride along question is in the ride
changes from one ride to the next. I would be difficult for me
ask VW about VW to understand a Jumbo Jet; although, both
can get me there. Where is the humor? It is the HA! HA!
Where is Poetic? It is in the line of A and B with C leaving.
With the crazy being, you saying, "Now I understand!" As the
singing Temptations say, "And, the beat goes on!"

Chapter VIII

Love -Sick -Crazy

Is this the plight?

of the love's bubble in flight

sickly riding the Atmos. . .-of-see-no-more,

and/or—

is this a crazy prelude about to burst before night?

Speak no Evil; Hear no Evil

In flirtatiousness, evil lurks in sexual foreplay.

This is about the ringed circus wanting to be laid.

79

First, there is the ring of engagement.

The game full of lying concealments,

In an effort to abort being an old maid.

In no time, there comes the ring of the wedding.

No one told us of the daily snoring in the bedding.

The enduring evil as we pretend not to hear.

This causes me before bedtime to drink a case of beer.

Whereas, the only satisfaction left is in the cheating.

Mixing a climax is the final ring call suffering.

From nowhere, there begins the shouting.

In real love, no evil is spoken.

This is of long-suffering with no vows broken.

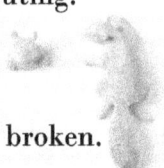

On holidays, there are the enjoyed squirrels chirping.

If you hear no evil; see no evil, you might end up stroking.

In the love sick crazy world, I am not just joking.

Kissing the only way to stop the fussing!

With mouth draped together, there is no cursing.

Up for air, there is the keep from choking.

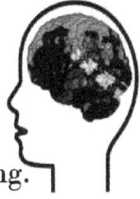

The longer you stay, the more the weirdness.

It's almost like dealing with a werewolf.

But without this crazy, life would be a bore.

When I can no longer take it, I will hit the door.

Weirdness, werewolf, and crazy do not mean weirdo.

Twisted Hearts of Love

Like the sweetness of hot apple pie lying on a table.

The warm wet mouth of love says, "You are invited!"

In the heat of the night, it was not only Eve along who ate the apple.

In the middle, "Twisted Hearts of Love" were enticed.

Love's house is ablaze and full of fire.

It is the smell of cedar that's a burning.

Opens the doors to fire's desire

This leaves "Twisted Hearts of Love" ever yearning.

After yearning, desire is about to explode.

This further twists the "Twisted Hearts of Love."

Each climax creates a readiness for a reload.

There is nothing like the here-in-above.

Love, Sick, Crazy Aftermath

In the pleasantry of daydreaming, those funny feelings of what-the-hell begin to creep into the empty crevices of the carcass. Life's living evidence is everywhere visible to the eye-shattering. Once the blinders are removed, for the most, there's the

received lightning bolt that strikes jolting in glimpses of reality. The derived energy erects to a stand up and stand out attention of the forgone and the at hand. Flowers and trees are no longer hiding the forest. There are monkeys swinging from one vine to another as to say, "No longer in the dark, but still let's swing!" Creatures of all types here and there in movement adorn the visible evidencing of the forest, and daydreaming is an in attendance event of reality. However, there is in the love, sick, crazy aftermath the still lingering pleasantry that's real whether a daydream or not. A move here or there tweaks to accent the pleasantry of feel good; here the memory of the in a night excursion wants now to jettison realty into the pleasant daydream –yearning again the relinquished climax. The pit in the stomach, the rise and fall of blood pressure, the stir craziness of intrusive thoughts, and the nervousness of overshadowing change seek a resolution that's in of itself earth shattering. In here, there is no sight of finality, and this too, as crazy as is, is a pleasantry that makes daydreaming, in the aftermath, a type of reality.

Speaking Nice is Easy

Even, dogs roll over to the voice of kindness.

Soft-speaking shows one to be harmless.

It is all in the calmness of the voice.

Don't say, "I cannot!" You do have a choice.

Try it! You, too, might like your niceness.

Slow Drag's After-Dance

In the heat of the night, love did a two step.

I knew that there was no way that I could sleep.

A final spin, hopefully, will not take me to an empty end;

Before, I head off to my den.

The one thing I hate is the hopeless counting of sheep.

Spin me around the dance floor once more and don't let me drop.

I refuse to let go, and I do not want to stop.

Until— I know how much you have to spend.

My pride or my DNA will not let me give nor lend.

You know; it takes money to shop.

Even the roller coaster ride cost money.

We can ride together, and I will let you call me honey.

I do not look at the height of how tall!

I caught Shorty, the Humpty Dumpty, before his fall.

Moreover, he was a fat-cat, but he too got stuck in my bunny.

Furthermore, O how— we enjoyed and danced the night away,

The fat-cat was happy; however, the bunny never receives an empty play.

In the morning, I hurried out the door

Looking good, feeling fine and spending at the store.

With plenty of Shorty's "Slow Drag After-Dance's, **okay**!

Falling in Love

The downward fall is of a caught me.

It happened around about the time I started to have tea.

My mate and I seemed to have jumped together.

In the spring time, we ride the blossoming wave of the weather.

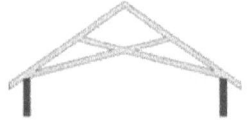

Falling in Love was easy, and now I see.

It is as if one jumped from the Empire State Building.

Half way down out the window came this ring,

"How are you enjoying the fall?

"I didn't know that the Empire State Building was this tall,

I retorted, I can no longer touch the ceiling."

However, "Fine——because I have not yet reached the ground."

In the mist of falling in love, I started to spin round and round.

Down and down, I further plunged.

I started praying for recoil and a landing sponge.

I could see the ground; I guess it is too late for a rebound.

Falling in love is a bitch; pretty much like landing in a ditch.

Some got trapped by Bozo the Clown or the West's Wick Witch.

The more you twist:, the deeper and tighter the mud.

Cleaning and removal take more than soap suds.

Oh, it fits; your head went into the hole, as did the ostrich.

Suck it up, you'll live; therefore, the fall was not all that bad.

Surely, you can handle the rest; you are a young lad.

I am old; my heart can no longer handle the recoil.

Love's rules are as cards in the book called Hoyle.

Cheer up my brother there is no reason to be sad.

As with everything in life, there are always at least two sides.

The cords of love are same for all: slip, slide or glide.

On the backside, I might not know your name.

This I do know; there is but one game.

Whosoever told you, Otherwise, they just lied.

Falling in Love is always the same for all.

At best, get a good view of the ground in the fall.

Hitting the ground is not a funny joke.

Whether rich, poor, or ordinary folks,

It is never about the bat and the baseballs.

I have a long shotgun with two bullets.

No matter how sweet, there are holes in donuts.

Many have drowned in the dive.

Even lovers come up now and then; get air to stay alive.

Beware! The rules of falling in love are not in any booklet.

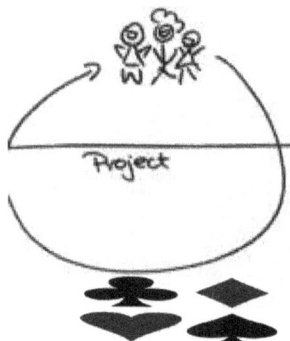

A Crazy Thought or Two

Reaching for the Rainbow melts in the attempted fancy of the mind under the triumph of love's desire in the underworld of the unclothed.

Reaching the top peak of the mountain, in of itself, is a feat divorced from another that sends reality, as fact, one must come down into the love or hate of the valley.

Love defies the gravitational restraints of nature's poles with love sending both headed toward the same hole in an amidst chance meeting.

The more I learn, the more I am convenience that I have never been in love; and if so, What the darn meaning of this love?

Caught a fly the other day and let him go; later killed the same fly; why is it the fly did not have sense enough to fly away and stay? You may say, "Oh, what the hell—that too sounds like love!"

Out of sight, out of mind is the quote, and love's greatest lie. Just as, truly you shall not die! What the hex? Who is it in that casket, the living dead? Close it! He might wake up and walk in the middle of the sermons. Wouldn't that be something to see?

Just scratch pad thinking. . .!

Love T-K-O

It is down and dirty. A turn of the page for the naughty receives the highlights. Tears of joy mourn now and then. Of the wane, it is often far spent. The correctness of grammar is only an accent. Behind and beneath the glamour, herein comes the finale. Hoop the Do and all that, who care about the fight; unless, it is a love's T-K-O!

We crossed the dessert at the end, just to end up on the beach, playing in the sand— all, for the craziness of love. Who cares about the warning, I know that a shark attack is in the eating. It is love, baby! Crabs' bones beat the hex out of dessert scorpions' soup any day. Might take a chance, here, and ride a whale and stand up on his back as a sail. Sound like a plan and could be another Love T-K-O!

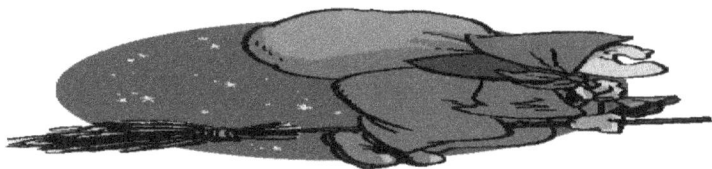

Come on, I'm off for more. . .!

Who Cares

It was last night that I had another love affair.

    She wears diamonds because I gave them as a present!

We love to style and profile on the Thoroughfare.

    Watching all you peasants!

I will not be blunt, but some would say you are a fool.

    Diamonds or whatever, in all honesty, "Who cares?"

How cool is cool when you have to pay to be cool?

    The black widow has a web she uses to ensnare.

Chapter IX

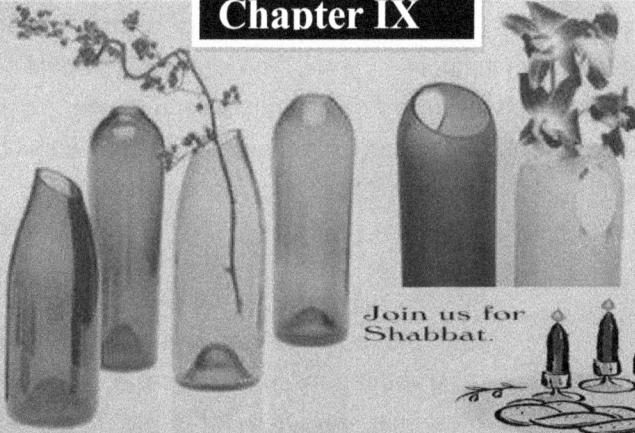

Join us for Shabbat.

Wine, Lies & Dine

THIS IS THE — BEST THING EVER!

Weekend

I told you the truth, but the wine you drank has you crazy; I am not a liar. I'm telling you the truth! I will cross my heart, and you know the rest, don't you?   Come now and eat, you know that there is nobody but you. Okay? That was just my personal trainer exercising me and teaching me about applying safe sex practices for you, baby. That's all that was— practicing so I would be good for you. It was not real

love like we have. Sex is only real with you. You work so hard, and I want to always be good for you; so, I practice to stay in shape for you; you do understand, don't you? You know that I would not put anyone before you; even, my dad comes second to you. That's like saying, "I will kill myself if I can't have you." And, that would be like you committing murder. You are not some murderer or a serial killer, are you?

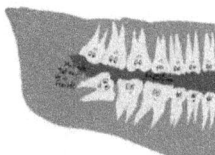

Just because you are rich, your money does not mean a thing about how I feel for you. I know that you are just like me; I will give you all my money just to be with you. You do feel that same way about me, do you? By the way, thank you for that money for my daddy's operation. He is not out of danger yet, but he would have died if he did not get that heart transplant yesterday.

Besides trying to be with you this weekend, I planned skydiving on tomorrow, but you know Dad has been sick—bad heart and all; he has not been able to work. We wouldn't dare ask you to pay for our playful little skydiving. Oh! You say you will. You are sweet; I might have another little treat for you a little later. How does that sound to you? By the way, I just talked to daddy today after he got his new heart; he says it is working fine, thanks to you. If there were enough room on the plane, I would ask you to dive with dad and I.

Oh! What the hex. I guess another glass of wine won't hurt you, would it? Fine, Oh, how fast time flies. Other girls would not look out for you, like I do.   It just occurred to me. Due to the lateness of the hour, we will not have time for the sex that I had planned for us from all the practicing I did.   But, you don't have to worry, I am going to try and get in a little more practice, and I'll be better than ever, and I promise you the whole week is going to be yours.

Baby, again, the whole weekend belongs to you and real loving, but you must let me keep practicing so that I can be your good girl, and I do know how you feel about dad. By the way, I do need about a grand so that I can pay for my practice exercise.   Don't worry, honey, I'll spend a little time with dad this weekend too —a day or so—at the hospital; hopefully, they won't need more money keeping that old heart they put into dad's stomach working. Silly, you know that the doctors want dad back at the hospital after he get some that wind out the sky.   You know, they pumped it up to where the heart supposed to fit. I know I can count you for more money, but you have done too much already; so, I am not going to ask you for more money. However, you could write me a check; oh, say, around seven thousand; you know me; I am not going to spend it; Oh, I am beginning to feel so sad.   The more I think about dad; the worst I feel.   Hopefully, dad will not start dying, but I know you would want me to pay the doctors to stop dad from dying, wouldn't you? You have never met my dear old dad,

but I know how you feel about him. I believe this is why I love you so much.

Every time you write a check, it just makes me cry. Now you know that I cannot tell a lie; you are the sweetest man I ever had. Before you, I thought dad was my Sugar-man. Here is a hug and a kiss because you are my new Sugar-man. From this point forward, I am going to just call you Sugar. You are really sweet! If you were in my place, I would give my last dime, too.

If something would happen to you, like bankruptcy or your oil wells went dry, I would hate the world for you.   Your wife could be just taking advantage of you spending all our money, and don't love you like I do.   I am about to cry again, Sugar! I love you so much; I just couldn't take it if something would happen to you.   Now, you know how I feel!   I have never said these things to anyone else!

Look at you, it is so easy for you to hand me a check, and I know what you are thinking; money isn't everything.   Don't forget, you are everything, Sugar. This is why I said what I told you before as we dined. I have always told you the truth, but you somehow are looking for lies. Can you promise me that you will never again think that I am laying to you, Sugar?   And, then again, if I was a liar, would I have told you that I use to be a bad girl.   Remember, I told you that the moneys you have given have made a good girl out of me. You believe me, don't you?

I really want to keep you here all night, but that would mess up the good girl image that you have paid making. Furthermore, I don't want your wife mad at you, either. For the weekend, send her to Alaska, moose hunting or something because I want you all to my selfish hunger getting as much of your sugar loving as I can, does you like that? And, I agree with you, money is not everything, so spend a couple of dollars and get rid of your wife and save the rest for me.

Your money has been used wisely by making me your good little girl, just like my day, and I cannot get enough of it, Sugar. Sugar, you are slick. You used your money to turn me into a good girl, and you are using your money to further hook me in your love. I kinda feel used, but don't stop because no has ever made me feel like you do. Go home; you need your rest for the coming weekend. I'll just be lying around are here with practice love, missing your real love, Sugar! I am your sucker, and I am going to do my best to suck as much love as I can out of you this coming weekend as humanly possible. I know you are excited too! Believe me, Sugar; my love is going to rip you dry with all of yours in my lovers' bank. Have you had a woman to wash your feet? Okay!
The weekend, Buy!

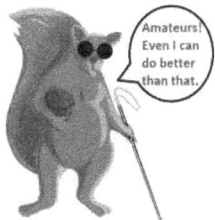

Amateurs! Even I can do better than that.

97

Watch Your Step

I'm telling you that it is not love; unless, it is blind.

The more that one sees, the more the lying.

What make you think that you are worthy to help?

Just because I am blind with eyes closed; I am not asleep!

Do I look as if I am dead meat for the dying?

One slip, then comes the autumn leaves of fall.

It came early in the morning right after nightfall.

In— slipped, a missed step that was not watched.

On my gun, I received another notch.

Watch your step, blind love is not for all!

LET'S EAT

Eating unlocks and satisfies the heart

It's like playing poker; the ace is the best hold card.

Isn't funny how joy comes from the center.

And— you want to know what's for dinner.

It's crazy; **BEWARE**, there is, occasionally, a fart.

On a date, this is why caviar is preferred to beans,

Which are designed to keep one strong and lean?

Love and a fart are not greatest combined delicacy.

The fish roe is caviar purging the inefficacy.

Just saying, doing my best to keep everything clean.

You know; I can get down and dirty.

Especially, when, it comes to Ms. Perdirty.

My eyes glitter awaiting the dessert to come.

All I'll say is— "Yuma, Yuma, and Yuma!"

I'm ready for the down, dirty, and under thirty.

It's the same fancy for guys and gals alike.

You know; the fine wine whets the appetite.

Win begins the crazy good feeling romantic arousal.

In the neurotic, it's our stimulus to be espoused.

Your teeth glister as stars, delightful and bright.

As, caviar's fish-roe sucks me into the swine's adore.

Of, course; she's too pretty and loving to be a whore.

Sucking on those oysters, I hope she doesn't choke.

Her mouth-watering, sweet smile is no hoax.

Let's eat outdoors — "How about a little more?"

Chapter X

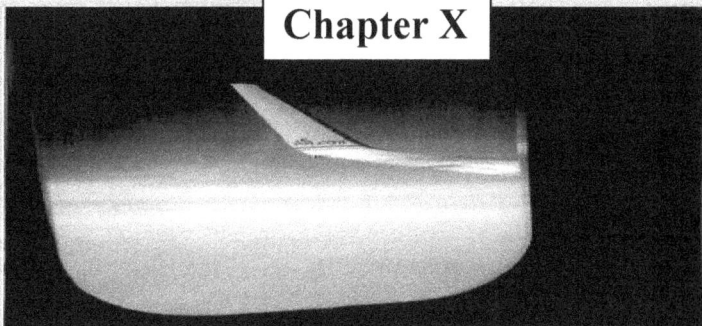

POETIC—CRAZY WINDOWS

Just love the window seat on an airplane when there is bad weather or a fool on the plane. I know you have heard the story about the "Thing-a-fied Lawyer." *There was a seasoned lawyer that purchased a new Bentley. He parked his Bentley in front his office to show to friends his new car. Lo and Behold! Just as he opened the door of his Bentley, a truck came along and took the left door of the car. Luckily, a policeman was behind the lawyer and saw*

every- thing. The lawyer jumps out of his Bentley screaming mad to the top of his voice. The police officer came to the rescue and said to the lawyer, "Stay calm, I'm here to help you." The lawyer replied, "You cannot help me, my Bentley will never be the same again!" The officer in a rebuke stated, "That just like you lawyers, all you lawyers care about are things." The lawyer asked, "What do you mean?" The police officer said, "You are worried about your Bentley and some missing door; what about your missing arm?" The lawyer screamed, "OH NO— MY ROLEX!" On the airplane you will do just fine; unless, you so happen to sit by a lawyer or the weather become turbulent.

Life's Window of Opportunity

From a series of "misunderstood" come the, "Did you Know!"

I was there, Johnny on the spot, "For Show!"

The King and Queen of the one breed.

They both got their wanted, fulfilling their desire's needs.

You see, and you know! Or, are you that slow?

BLACK & WHITE

Commingled

The truth of one is the no more wanting to hear.

What will it be: a Black or White lace?

It's the difference of the antelope and the deer.

Human is really the only race.

103

Flipping the flop, let us rock to this exciting new jingle.

I am moved by the lyrics coming from the "Get Together!"

Pleasing and satisfying are the notes commingled.

Inside, it doesn't matter as to the weather.

I heard a sermon about God's children here are one,

All are Welcome And God is no respecter of persons.

Looked in the church for races, and there were none.

It's almost as if God adopted stepsons.

The jingle made us feel good, "We are the Children!"

It is all about the differences that we are to make.

JINGLE

The glass ceiling stopped us from becoming mandarins.

I guess the only acceptable commingling is in the wedding cake.

Window High Love

Hi! I just moved into #10!

Oh hi! I love your floor-length arched windows!

Anything above the #2 wear a parachute.

Wear it, as if, it is your player's suit.

Believe me, above #2 the air is mighty thin.

Jumping out windows above #2 has been never a win.

Keep your eyes open as you shoot!

Window high love has caused many to jump and run.

Flying out of windows is really no fun.

I can't help it that you got caught.

And, at the same time, you bought?

105

Yes, her name was Nun; she said, "Buy or get none!"

You bought, got none, and jumped from a window,

Say what? You left your pants and the rest of the doe.

Oh, ID in your wallet, I know— waiting the return.

Window jumped and you still have not learned.

Next, you will tell me that Nun is not a whore!

You say no because you got caught by her father.

Okay, Why did you not ask father, where's the altar?

Nun and Father, do you see? No need to jump!

Look, there in the mirror, is that a bump or a lump?

Paid Ms. Nun; jumped from window for a lifesaver.

Crazy Window Philosophy

A man committed a horrendous crime, but deems to be mentally ill at the time of the crime. This man was sentenced and sent to the institution for the criminally insane. A deputy was given charge of that despicable excuse as a human being. He was carried to the institution where the deputy took him to the second floor for residence. Outside, it has begun to rain. Upon leaving and arriving at his car the deputy discovered that he had a flat tire on his transportation. In the process of change the flat, the deputy lost all tire lugs in mud. The deputy immediately raised his hands up toward the sky and

shouted, "Oh, Lord—what am I going to do now?" The insane man on the second floor placed in the institution shouted from his window, "Take a lug nut off of each of your other tires and secure that tire. When you get to a parts house, buy more lugs, stupid!" The deputy retorted and asked, "I thought that you were crazy?" The insane man replied, "I might be crazy, but I am not stupid, Stupid!"

Chapter XI

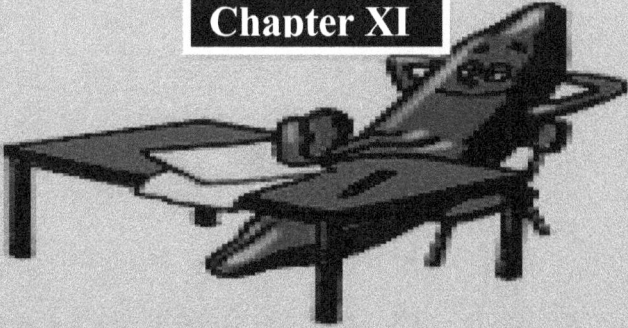

The Crazy Imaginative Hang Ups

In a view, there is the jealousy—the strange inner enemy— connected with the pictures that remind us always of the relinquished. The enemy—created or real—gets our attention fogging our pathways of sagacity. There is here the split asunder as the inner equilibrium makes the hounds howl and the dogs bark. One believes that he makes better music than the other in the chamber of the crazy imaginative hang ups. Both make hungry the jealous nature of the imaginative carnivorous inner beast. The craziness of these tugs away at one another the same way that lies and egos in the paradox need kindness and truth. Here we go again, and asked by

another, "Which one makes the best music? The resounding answer came as, "The one you hear!"

Love Only Party Girls

Daddy said, "I am leaving my wealth to stable family man!"

"I will divide between you and your brother is the plan."

Either of you has to have a stable marriage for a period five years.

Right away, I imagined a life of torching tears.

Whereas, I would have to give up all the party girls I ran.

Imagine, I have to give up all that fun and sex.

This will drive me to a living wreck.

Can I trust my brother to take all and then share?

Because, getting a party girl to change is rare.

Even, daddy might end up as her next.

I need a new book on this one guy and gal thing.

No longer a swinger, did you say I have to give up my Bling?

I am sure that daddy's money is worth the sacrifice.

I love my party girls, and to give all up is a hell of a price.

I know, I can change daddy's thinking by getting him a fling.

Bad Connection

Afterward, there was sorrow etched on the face.

Was it a lie or something else that created the case?

Two bubbles of air between the bobble head.

They lay in bed away from the moment of the dead.

Lost communication created a sweet embrace.

My battery ran down, and I had to recharge my phone.

111

Of course, I was not looking at porn!

A bad connection or battery down can happen to anyone, you know!

I could have lied and told you that it was because of the snow.

Come here and forget about that bad connection and get warm.

The Annoying Difficulty

How did it happen? You know: the time of being trapped away from the present. It was in that period of unprofitability where sleep was a lost over nothing. This was the preoccupation with the foolish in the most awkward moment of growing. It happened suddenly as if an avalanche swooped down covering the body with beautifying snow. In a period of unrest, there was this psychological block, as of a prison, which restricted utter rational movement. The annoyance of the whole ordeal was exasperating, to say the least, deflating the ego to a decomposing vegetable. The sharp aggressiveness of intellect is now a struggle, seeking equilibrium. Since no one knows what this infers, try this on for size: *Unwanted Love as a Hang Up*.

The Morning After

It is not the pill, but an awakening from sleep.

At first, I should have left along the sheep.

However, it is good that I am awake at last.

O what foolishness and drama that is now of the past.

There is much in the "What you sow you will reap."

There is not worst than the cultivation of false illusions.

They will fog you head with all sort of delusions.

Have you crawling up a tree like an Acorn Weevil,

Or, in cotton field sing the Boll Weevil.

Once was a fool is only a conclusion.

Get married and then fall in love.

Don't let yourself get caught like baseball in a glove.

The most one should give away is a hug.

The rest is for pay marrying the old lug.

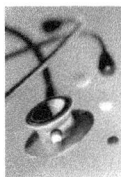

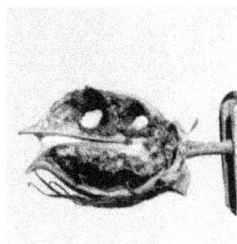

The morning after, he will see you as his dove.

Connoisseur

Beyond the hang-ups, there is the connoisseur—the

POTLUCK DINNER

expert of taste. The application is to everything (i.e., fine wines, foods, music, guys & gals, and others). This is not a money measure; it is either it is, or it is not. The funny thing about being a connoisseur is that the expert cannot be fool by imitations, and the lying talk of snake-oil nonsense cannot persuade to the contrary. The connoisseur just knows; there are no classes that align with perfection. The best of the best is evident in quest

thereof from beginning to end. The escape is of the fact no matter what; it is never there all of the time.

The Honesty in Lying

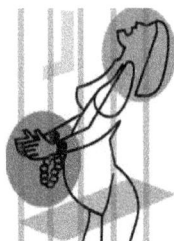

If it were true, I saw Spaceship; could I tell you?

The honesty of truth has to be a lie that keeps me out of the zoo.

It is the keeping of secrets that allows the other to lie.

For, if it were not for the lies, many would or could die.

Was it the truth or a lie that destroyed the Sioux?

The point being is the knowing what to say and when.

Like having the name Fake, but in reply, "My name is Ben!"

With the giving of a humorous smile and grin, I say, "Hi!"

Will it be Jake or Ben that says, "Bye?"

This is just another way we justify lying to win.

After all the small falsehoods, we, all, think ourselves to honest.

This is despite the truth that we conveniently harnessed.

Here in the sanctity of expediency!

It will be off tomorrow that we erect the decency.

The honesty in lying today is the only candidness.

Chapter XII

CONNECT WITH RESPECT

Social Media Exploration

Love's New Topic

It seems like the internet goes to Swift.

It is the skimpy wearing that's causing the rift!

Whereas, the old man pinches for a dip,

Placing the cup's dip in his lip.

NO ME DIGAS

Swift bends causing the head to spin.

It is the playboy that gets the win.

Leaves dipping, boyfriend, gives a bottle of gin.

On his face, there is the smurk of a hilarious grin.

Dwelving into Swift, it is Swift to give the gift.

Taking over, he gives swiftly with a lift.

A dollar or two get a ride on the blimp.

Up, up and away, one needs a rift.

In the fall, it is for fun and love.

Hitting the ground is a sure glove.

When it hurts, it's a massage—the sexual rub.

In the set free, we fly away like doves.

The Internet Ride

Here as to the taste and preference, the ride is faster than any man made roller coaster. Along the way— there is screaming, lying, and all out laughter of seriousness, wacky, and crazy in the name of entertainment. Beyond lightning speed, it is here before my eyes for an inspection. The eyes flutter as to the float of the ride seeing the many amazing, instantaneous sites along the way. One to the next and more as we go! The journey has no end but furthers the quest for more. The next bend is always a mind opener to the thrill of the imagination. The stop is only to the "I want or need no more."

Yet— this is the only a momentary pause of a surfer on the wave of light, which did not disrupt the links. The quest for more is of a push of the button as if there was no pause as to the riding surfer on the lightning ride. As always, this is an every beginning anew.

The Pretense of the Internet

Looking at pretense, could this my friend be also my enemy?

Or, is this a spy in time that will live in infamy?

In waves, the smiles and the faces do tell lies.

With a loss of reality, O' how, in this pretense, time flies,

Absorbing into the cloud of web 3.0— the whole anatomy!

It is here that friends and enemies are as close as the other.

There is always a spy pretending to a brother or a lover.

In the pretense, you will never know what's going to be next.

At any time, one can become part of the front page's text.

Eyes are everywhere—even, under the cover.

Touching others seems like a friendly game of matrix.

Or, is this too a pretense before something goes ballistic?

Some say that this is just the school of the new day.

Presence aside, you know that someone has to pay.

It's the games we play making us all somewhat pseudo-artistic.

About the Author

Sherman A. Jones is an accomplished author, and business person with several academic degrees, certificates, certifications, licenses, and memberships.

Degrees:

(1)   Radio & Broadcasting,
(2)   Electronics,
(3)   Theology,
(4)   Legal Studies (Bachelor's Degree), and
(5)   Higher Education (Master's Degree Teaching Adults on the College Level).

Certificates, certification, and license:

(1)   Hand on Switch Mode Power Supply Troubleshooting.
(2)   National Institutes of Health (NIH) Office of Extramural Research,
(3)   Federal Communication Commission, and
(4)   Graduate Degree in Online Teaching

Memberships:

(1)   Alpha Beta Kappa Honors Society
(2)   Kaplan University Student Military Association (KUSMA Alumni
(3)   Disabled American Veteran (DAV).

Owner of the Company and Publisher of this book and others.

www.ingramcontent.com/pod-product-compliance
Lightning Source LLC
Chambersburg PA
CBHW030012110426
42741CB00032B/477